LIFE OF LOTUS

Kartikay D Pawar

TO THE ONE
WHO CREATED THIS BEAUTIFUL WORLD

&

TO THE ONES
WHO SHOWED ME HOW TO LIVE IT

1
COMMUNICATIONS

2
BEAUTY

3
STRENGTH

4
WISDOM

LOVE OF LIGHT & NIGHT

6
DUTIES

7
SPIRITUALITY

8
AMBITIONS

1

COMMUNICATIONS

MY SONG

These tables
These forks and knives
Coffee and food
It feels same every time,

These tables with chairs
These tables with people everywhere
But with me, it's just me and the chair.

I wish you were here.

TEARDROP

Went against the fear
But coming into the year with tears.
He said don't worry my dear
You are more than what you hear,
I went against the fear.

Every teardrop is counted
Every teardrop is seen
Through the eyes of the stars.
Once you open your eyes
The light will be seen,
So that you can go
Against the fear.

IT FALLS

We were born in the night
To shine in the day,
I was there watching
Learning as a knight every day.

Rain falls like every day
Bringing sorrow with it
But lessons within,
It will be over in no time
Like it was not there ever in time.

MERCURY

As kids, I use to think
My sick days are over,
As kids, I didn't realize
Real bad days are on the horizon.

Now I don't think
As a naive adult
What future holds,
As I found peace
In what God holds.

I seek today
I seek the most out of it,
That's where happiness lies
That's where the truth lies.

LOOK ABOVE TIMES CHANGING

I learned with time
To respect others what they are doing
& To respect me even more
For what I am doing.

Time has the power
The most underrated power
Which can turn everything around
And leave you on ground or
Take you up above.

RAHUL

No matter if I know
Anything or not,
No question if I remember
Anything or not
No matter what,
I know
Even in my sleep
You are always there
That you are still there for me.

It doesn't matter
I am here
& You are over there,
What I know is
I am always there
That I am still there for you.

LOVE/LIFE

Love is everything
Believe it or not,
Love someone
Whether it's you or me.

I want thy love
It makes my day.

Believe it or not
I will make you mine,
Whether it's you or god
I will be yours
& Glory will be mine.

I want thy love
So, glory will be mine.

CONNECTION

I felt profoundly connected
Through the clouds
By the ocean
With the air which shrouds
I saw where it all started.

I made a deal of grace
With the ultimate beauty,
I will make the world better
If not much then at least a bit sweeter.
He asked me
Can u overcome sufferings?
I said
As long as I have u
There are no sufferings.

ACROSS THE OCEANS

I was kicked alone
In the middle of darkness
Across the oceans
To the loneliness,
When I needed u most
My everything
I was left all alone
In the world which I once knew.

GAL WE ARE AT PEACE

Now I felt
How its like to be free,
Now I felt
As I asked you for your forgiveness
For the mistakes I did.

I did my work
Whether I receive forgiveness
Or not, I did my karma,
Now I am free
because I have learned.

I CAN HEAR HIS VOICE
IN MY HEAD

You meet people to realize
They love something like you do,
You know people to realize
They are afraid of things like you are,
You love some people when you realize
They also lost something or someone
Like you have.

ENTER

A half heart is always a question
Which searches for answers
Weak enough to find the solution
That the most powerful weapon is the heart
When it comes in full throttle.

THERE IS A WAY AROUND

She is the loudest of the storms
One of the fragile you could think,
Escape was my answer
Peace was my weapon.

Nobody warned about the sign,
About the road
Which I walked long enough,
When I look back, I see a naive child
Unaware of the consequences.

IN THE AIR

Love is the most valuable thing
The thing which has life
More than you can think.

Help yourself
Love yourself
Live for the earth
It is what giving you love.

AROUND YOU

When you wanna cry but
Don't wanna let others down,
When you wanna run away but
Your strings won't let you go.
That's the moment
You let yourself know
Faith is where god shines
Love is where God resides.

ROOTS

Love finds its way
Just remember
If it has to come
Love will find its way.

So I see you coming again
Back into my life,
I see you have changed
But still, you haven't changed in there.

GIRL, HEAL ME WITH YOUR SMILE

You make me walk on this road
You make me climb on that wall
Who knows what's next but
Who cares as long as you are there.

BELLS

Surrender yourself to God
And he shall lift you up to the sky
Open up your heart to him
And he will lit the whole sky.

TELL ME HOW ?

If your heart is not broken
Then how you can know
What it feels like to have a heart,

If your success is gifted
Then how you can know
What it feels to have real success
Which is earned.

LAST ENCOUNTER

You took my kindness for weakness
Without knowing the beast in me
Which is silent, not dead.

You took my love for granted
Thinking its endless
But everything is bound to end.

You then crushed it
The heart which I gave you
Into ashes which are still there,

Not for you
But for me
To remind, it was a mistake
That I loved you.

2

BEAUTY

HEART IS NOT A MACHINE

Fool your mind
Don't fool your heart
Mind play games
Don't let it play with your heart,

He will play with you
He may use you
But never let him take you
Away from you
Never let him fool you.

YOU - OUR TIME

The reasons are not necessary
Sometimes silence is what required,
She said: what about the promises?
What about those feelings we shared?
He said: those promises made me realize
I am not the one but you who deserves more.

Back to your laughs
Back to your tears
This is what I want to remember,
Happy times which we shared.

I saw in and out of you
Now I can see myself from head to toe,
Times are changing
But it's you who turned me
It's our time which changed me.

TOGETHER

Give me strength in my flesh
To climb the mountains,
Instead of coming closer
They become tougher & tougher
As I climb higher & higher.

Air is not helping
Your name is,
They call you with different names
I call you with love
I call you by faith.

MAX

When I first saw her
It felt like the heart
Came out & shouted to my face
She is my Rushmore!!!
Same like that guy...

It may not be 1998
But it was undoubtedly 2016,
Too much magic feels
In a moment to work out.

She might not be the one
But definitely, she was
My Rushmore, though for a moment
It was a magical one.

FAULT

Girl don't forget how great you are
Girl I want u to remember
Things do happen
Things will happen
It's not your fault.

It may turn a kind soul bad
Girl I want u to remember
Don't let it rot your soul
It's not your fault.

VENUS

She goes where she belongs
In the wild forest, into the wild sea,
There she goes where she belongs
To the moon & back to the sea.

She is the craziest I have known
The one you don't wanna leave,
She is the one
Who makes the world less mad &
There she goes.

STARS

Her lips were like wildest dreams
Among the stars, brightest ever.
I could have kissed her all night
Still, her lips would not shed light.

NOT FOREVER, NOTHING LASTS FOREVER

I

It will rain
But it won't rain forever,
Sun will shine again
But it won't shine forever.

You were born here
To live, not to sweat
But to sweat to have a life.

||

I saw them go down
As you achieve arrogance
Everything goes down.

You got the fire
Inside you, To preserve
Not just you but all,
Keep it burning
Not to burn
But to preserve.

SUBMIT YOURSELF

How can I grow
Without storm
When no seed
Can grow without rain,

How can I love
Without sacrifice
When no being
Can love without pain.

MAYBE NEVER WILL

I say your name
More than you remember
I loved you
More than you felt.

Girl don't look at me
Look in you
You won't see me
Cause I was never there.

GRAVITY

Look through my eyes
You will see the cracks within,
Look through my eyes
And you will see the beautiful world
You could ever imagine.

NOT A DREAM

I will never let you go
Even if you beg me
I won't let you go.

You are my hero
You have always been my hero,
That's what changed me
That's what made me K.P.

You are not a dream
You are the person
Who makes other people's ideas
Come true
You are more than a dream
Wake up.

ITS RAINING, NON-STOP

Everything is so fragile
Which seems to break
Nothing is organic nowadays,
Neither love nor people
It looks so plastic on the outside
& So fragile from the inside.

BEAUTIFUL TRUTH

Glass full of beauty
Waiting for you to sip it down
That's life calling for you
Filled with tears of joy in you.

KID

It's not about your life
It's about life itself,
Where you take part in
Where you try to have a piece of it
It's not about you, it's about life.

ENDLESS

Lights running down the streets
Like its searching for something,
Lights reaching down to my soul
Like its there to tell me something.

THE DARK ROAD GETS LONGER

Silent places hide violent echoes
With curses hidden in the air
For the land to be free
But still being trapped.

Women's tears heard in the air
With pain to be felt
For those who do evil
But still being free.

End puts everyone on the back
Each life taken has to be paid
Your deed shall be counted
Upon which you shall pay.

OO2O

I was trying to end it
For straight 30 minutes,
Come in she said
It will be alright.

At last, I was afraid
She might fall in love,
As I didn't reach the end
As she already did
Like too many.

I stepped out
With my chin up
With my music on
It was more than alright.

FLY

I am afraid of the obvious
But more than that
I am afraid I will burn
Not you but myself
Cause you are more than
what I can hold,

You are a bird
Destined to be free,
I am a cage
Which won't agree.

GOODBYE

There are choices which stars make
& Then there are choices within it
Which we choose.
There are consequences
Which are to be endured,
For better or for worse
There are choices which we choose.

3

STRENGTH

I REMEMBER

A girl
Who can take anything,
A girl no matter how fragile
Is who can stand again n again
Without breaking apart.

The girl I met
On street of Meserole,
The girl who was tight as a rock
The one who was soft like an angel.

DO IT RIGHT

It's not one
It's more than that,
What you do carries on
What you learn
You just take it on
On to the next
The life which seems one
It's not, it's more than that.

FRAGILE LIGHT

I guide you
There is a pit ahead,
I enlighten you
To be smart
But I forget how he can change
When he doesn't want to,
I forget how God can help
When he doesn't help himself.

I never give up
To help you, to save you
I never stop
For what positivity can save
But how can I see you lose
All you have worked for
How can I forget
What promises you lived for.

MARS

Every teardrop has a past
Every teardrop is for the future,
No one shall have revenge
For the things which are there
To be forgotten.

HE-SHE

He is not the one who gives up,
He is not the one who gets satisfied
What he is born with,
The one who looks up to Greatness
Despite the struggles with it,
The one who sees those as
Opportunities,
He is the one who becomes great.

YOUR WORDS AREN'T CLEAR / LIKE YOUR MIND

You think you have
Broken heart,
You think that is the most painful thing
You don't think
Broken soul
Is the most painful thing,
You don't think
You are not the only one.

Sometimes I feel
Nobody has idea
How it feels
& Sometimes I think
That they are out there,
They know
How it feels.

WE WIN, ALWAYS

Only strong survive, true that
Not to forget, a soft heart is what makes us
Not to mention, a smart mind makes us live,
Let them know, who are we
Let them know, by a smile.

EVERYWHERE

Every teardrop is watched
Like a drop of rainfall,
A drop of grief
Which is observed,
Whether you see it or not
But you might feel
You are watched.

COME BACK NOT FOR YOURSELF BUT FOR OTHERS

When they say
Will he come back?
    You have to speak
    By showing up,
    I was destined to come back
    Giving up is not in my blood,
    It's contagious
    I stay away from it.

    You have to crave giving
    Like we want for love,
    Let go some of your stuff
    At least some,
    It's not going downhill
    It's letting go to help others.
Why
    To grow together
    There's love.

I

ULTIMATE WEAPON

The one who climbs
The impossible,
One who runs
Like the wind,
Who loves
Like God
Its the human spirit
Which can absorb anything
Like an infinite hole.

II

ULTIMATE BULLET

I wonder if I fail
What will happen,
I cry if no one loves me
What will happen,
When I look up
He gives me the source
He gives me the hope.
Now I know
I will be fine,
The world will be fine
Cause I have hope.

ITS TIRING

When I feel that air, I don't feel good
Cause its made of all that stuff
Which is not good,
Negativity surrounds me
I am here to love,
With all that bullshit
How can I be loved?

HOW FAR YOU CAN TAKE IT ?

Your love shall be tested
Like nature test its animals.
Run from it, hide from it
Or face it just for once.
Your love shall be pressed
To make it stronger
Your love shall be tested.

ENOUGH OF ME

I wish I can be more me
I will put more
Smile & love
I hope I could do me,
Maybe I will find someone just like me.

Those who come in the way
Will meet with fury & anger,
It all comes around from love
But don't mistake love with my weakness
Cause my love is my weapon,
My love is my strength.

LIGHTROOM

He might have put me in this cell
With bars & walls around me
But only to make me learn,
Just to make me strong
So that I can be free, forever
When the time comes.

DETOX

I am like a rabbit
Swimming through the sharks
With uncertainty & unkind,
Running from something
Fighting for nothing.

Like birds
Flying away from their sorrows,
I am lonesome
Trying to learn

To stay on the ground
Not to fly over much &
Not to drown underground.

CAN YOU SEE IT ?

Suppressing doesn't work always,
What's inside of you, let it come out
For good or for bad,
In the end, it will be good for you
And for the people around you.

HANDS

Why people move behind
When they have a road ahead,
Maybe they are afraid of what lies ahead
Maybe all they did was wrong,
The wrong road which is now left behind.

AN OCEAN APART

They say its pain that teaches you
But its the love in pain
That turn things around
Not pain itself but love.

COLDER THAN YOU THINK

The calmer the road
Useless it is to walk,
No one has achieved good
Without walking the treacherous path.

YOU HAVE SEEN ME SHINE, YOU HAVEN'T SEEN ME CRY

I am not tired of sufferings
But tired of being strong,
Am tired of standing again
And again to get punched down.
Am not tired of failing
Am tired of trying
Again and again.

My life became upside down
I took hard punch straight
On my jaw.
It brought me down
It got touched by the hands
Of devil
But I am gonna turn this tragedy
Into miracle by the hands
Of the lord.

4

WISDOM

LIGHT WILL PASS

The walls fall down
Sky opens up,
When you believe things will change
Sun shows up.

Light gives you therapy
It will heal your wounds,
It shall heal your soul
You will be you again
But a better self
A better being.

That's the purpose
You will get it
Not now then later,
Light shall pass
Through you
It will bounce back
To the world
Through you.

LIFE IS A ROAD

I

Life is a road
Neither short nor long
But a bittersweet journey like the song,
Look behind you
Look ahead of you
Its how you see
Not how you get
Life is a road.

||

I look behind me to realize how much I
changed,
I look in front of me to see how much I have
to change.
There is an invisible power
Behind me
Beside me
Before me
& In me.
There is a power which tells me
Keep the faith, the road leads north,
There is a power which tells me
Life is a road which leads north.

SMILE

If you learn to swim
Learn to swim in life,
If you learn to dance
Learn to dance in life.

Otherwise, in the storm,
You will be shattered
In melody, you will be senseless,
Life is not a box
Its an ocean of love and salt.

UNTITLED

It's not about controlling nature
It's about controlling yourself,
So that God can connect with you
Not for himself
But for you.

JUPITER

We crave what we don't have
We are blind for what we have,
Endless search out there
For what we have in here.

For every kiss we share
It lasts hours,
For every hate we share
It lasts forever.

Love comes out of life
We will be alright,
If love is what we aim for
Then only we will be alright.

WE ARE AT WAR

No situation shall dictate our results
No outcome shall become disappointing,
As long as we thrive for good
As long as we strive for better
We should never quit, never.

LIKE A MELODY IN THE BRAIN

He was packing his bags
The stuff which was scattered
Around the room,
Like a melody in the brain
He looked out
Through the windows of the mind.
I felt comfort,
The comfort which was long gone
I was myself once more
As he - the negative self
Was not there anymore.

Came back to where it all started
In the mind
With a blessing placed by the one.
In the flight thinking about it
About the last day spent
NYC gave me the light.
Light of the time about to come
I saw the light as I bumped into it
After taking the wrong train twice,
He gave me the new route
As I gave him the faith
I felt the other side of the rain
Like a melody in the brain
Like a melody in the brain.

DEPART

The true discovery comes with loneliness
It leaves you all alone all empty
In the way of sacrifices
Not to give you greatness
But to make you great.

K.P

The Light Will Shine
Through The Darkest Clouds.

TRUST IT.

Nothing teaches you more than life itself
Once you open your arms
Life will build bridges for you,
Not to go across
But to go beyond,
Which is unseen
Which is unheard
Just open your arms.

CREATURE

Don't feel that much
That makes you forget,
Don't change others so much
That you forget to change yourself
For the time which is there to touch.

AFTERMATH

Certain things which are better forgotten
Certain things which you can't change
But some are there for you to feel
So you can be free, in time.

I asked myself is it worth it
To go through all this,

Time which is endless
In time you might escape
But will you be truly free?

I SEEK

I seek to find strength
Strength to fight the darkness
Inside me,
I seek to help
Those out there & those
Inside me.

LOOK CLOSELY

I was born in darkness
To shine in the light,
They can take everything but
God in life.

Sometimes healing lies in aching
Joy lies in tears,
Sometimes it's better to forgive
Not just them
But the pain in here.

See what lies beyond
Though ocean seems to end
There is a land
After horizon and beyond.

YOU HAVE THE POWER

How can u escape
What is meant for you
To face, to feel
For good or for bad
What is meant for you
You can't escape,
No Camel no Hennessy
Can help like what you can.

TIME IS LIFE

TIME - IS OUR ENEMY

Time will drag you
Against your will,
It's better to accept it
Time won't stop for you.

In time you will feel pain
In time you will realize
You are one of us
Time is no different for you.

Time - is our Saviour

It is our friend
Who makes us feel
The beauty of life,

It is our friend
Who saves us from sorrow
The way of showing future.

Time - is Limited

It is bittersweet
As it is limited,
Embrace it with love
To make full use of it.

GO ALL IN

In creativity
You bleed every day
You bleed all alone,
No one will be there to help
But yourself.

Pull yourself together
And keep on moving,
They will walk beside you &
Laugh at you, mock at you
They will do everything they can
To stop you.

Keep your head up, don't let them
Shape you.

LOOK-UP

What if, not backward I move forward
What if, my ignorance becomes wisdom
I won't be with you,
I will be watching you from above.

VAYU

I ask the mighty God
God of air, to bless me with speed,
Not to run away from the dark
But to cover me with light.

POSITIVE VIBES

Positive vibes
Don't think twice
Keep the dark out
Cause we live in the light.

ME

My DNA Speaks For Itself
I Speak For My Life Myself
I Don't Speak For The Karma
My Karma Speaks For Itself.

YOU

PURITY, I Build It Inside Me.
LOYALTY, I Pray It Inside Me.
LOVE, Is What I Hustle For.
RESPECT, Is What I Live For.

LOVE OF LIGHT & NIGHT

TO THE STARS

Don't look below
That's what time has buried,
Look above
That's what time has for you.

I

GO FIND ANSWERS

Why you put chains on me
When all I want
Is to set everyone free,
Why you cast me out
When all I want
Is to be around.

II

HE TAUGHT ME

Like sun who doesn't differ
When spreading light,
Don't let yourself
Differ when spreading the love.

REDEMPTION

I left abruptly
Thinking it was right
Until I realized it wasn't
It's been many years in the moonlight.

I set the bird free
So did me,
I let myself loose
So that she feels
That she has won
That she was right.

His shoulders became light
His soul finally saw the light.

<u>SUN</u>

A new sun will shine
It shall wipe out the dust of the past
It shall bring the light like never before.

MOON

There is no other love
Purer than your love,
Which nourished me
All this time from the start.
There is no other love
Which can heal &
Make me strong,
There is no other love
Warmer than you ma.

LET IT FLOW

You have to first endure fear
To become fearless,
Sometimes lessons are learned
From the opposite,
Sometimes life takes you
In the wrong direction
To make you walk on the right.

HE IS COMING

Watch me do things
Which you wished I couldn't do,
Watch me grow
Like never before,
Love me now
Because now days are changing
It won't be like before.

OMKAR

Brother
Oo my friend
Stand by me
Like you use to do
Like we use to be
Standing with each other,
We didn't worry
Of Storms
Of Sorrow
We were always there
For each other,
My friend
Be there for me
Like you use to
Stand by me.

EVOLUTION

Evolution is a part of life
Some welcome it
Some reject it, while
Some who are stupid enough
Run from it.

IT WON'T BE TENDER

Sunset takes away what it has given you
So you could learn to shine through the night,
For the morning which shall come
Will be brighter for those who fight.

JENNIFER

Though we have to depart
For the life which we have to follow,
We will meet again
This or the other time
Which awaits us
In a land far far away.

SHORT STORY OF SURVIVAL

Roots were always there
But I found water over here,
It was hidden
In the name of faith
Like gems hiding
In the midst of chaos.

GIRL CALLED JACQUELIN

In the city of sins
She gave me shelter
She gave me food,
In case of adversity
She still didn't cut me loose.

Maybe I failed her
But there shall be time
Where I will repay her
With kindness like her eyes.

JOY- IN TEARS

Its been a long time
Since the last time I came,
Now I am here
I feel like everything has changed.

I looked around
I saw myself wandering around,
Now here I am
A man not just with experiences
But with sufferings
But still, I made it this far
Here I am.

That day I felt things
Things which are rare
Which is uncommon to perceive,
That day I knew
It was not rain
But someone
Bursting into tears
Tears of joy
As he saw me,
It was not rain
It was tears of joy.

In the midst of darkness
In the noise of the sound
I saw the light of joy
As it was not rain
It was tears of joy.

YOU ARE THE ONE (WHICH I CAN'T HAVE)

Where do you go
When you are not yourself,
Where do you go
To seek what you need
But to only find what you want

What you will do
When the lights go off,
What you will do
When you see your true self
But not the one you threw lights on.

FOXEY LADY (A TRIBUTE)

Her mind is like fire
Burning through everything,
Her mind is like air
Changing from this to that
She loves me like no one has before
She loves like a FOXEY LADY.

BLUE

I can't make you fall
In love with me,
All I can do is love me
But love you more.
I wish you could see
What you are looking for
It's not out there
It's in me.

ASTRO

Tiny dots in the sky
Which are connected to make me wonder,
Tiny dots in the sky
Which can spark life like thunder.

DON'T SEARCH OUTSIDE, ITS IN YOU

There was a calm feel
Feel with no sound,
Felt like space with no time
Calmness, it was scary.

Sometimes its calmness
Which scares the most,
There was a time
It was darkness
Which frightened me the most.

At this moment
Darkness is your foe
Next moment
It can be your friend,
Once you accept it
You have gone too far, my friend.

No matter where you go
The light will follow you
Cause light is not found at a place
Its found in you.

FIREFLIES

For how long one can give light
For what it will provide?
Have you ever thought
Why fireflies die
So young in the times.

Those who provide light
Often gets left behind.

1995

I shall rise from the ashes
To shine like the sun
You have never seen.

5

DUTIES

इंक ओम्कार

Lord forgive me
For the sins I did,
Oo lord bless me
For the things, I should do
For the people of you.

You call me
From all temples
I go wherever you go
Cause I just see you
You call me
And I go.

For the people who cross by
I only bring love,
No matter how they are
I keep up the light.

Lord bless me,
For love, I should give
For the person, I want to be.

TRACKS

No pain is more than
What we deserve,
No joy is exalted from
What we are.

No rain can wipe
Our knight,
Like no fire can burn
Our light.

IT IS TIME

Don't run from rain
It is there for you to learn,
No matter where you go
It won't go away,
Don't get tired
As it won't go away
Until you learn.

I see the rainbow
Shine, up high
I see the struggles
Fade, far behind.

REAL HUMANS

Birds are singing
Bees are hovering over clover,
The sky is showering love
& Humans are crying over nothing.

There are hustlers
There are lovers fixing hate,
I am learning from them
As real humans making a change.

FOR YOU

I see myself in the mirror
And I see u all
Because I am no one
If there is none of you all.

There's nothing I want from you
I just want to help all,
As in return, I know
You will help the rest
& Then I will be in peace
Then I will be in rest.

SATURN

The process shapes you
The process makes you,
You can't skip it
You can't run from it
If you did,
You haven't made it.

KILL THEM

Forgiveness shall be given
Given to the worthy enough
But will be given at a price,
The price that is 'limit.'

Battles have to be fought
Not in the world,
Battles have to be fought
Inside of you.
Battles have to be won
Not by weapons
But forgiveness by you.

THE TIDE

I might cry, not that I am weak
But to feel that I am still a man,
I shall find a way, not for revenge
But to feel peace, in forgiveness.

PULL IT OUT

They are not outside the circle
True haters always lie near you,
Push them out
Before they ruin you.

Jesus, Allah, Om
Guide me
Pull the devil out of my life
But I know you won't,
So give me strength
To tackle it myself.

ELECTRIC

Time which is there to touch
Time which is made to feel
Not to walk through
But to make it real.

CONFUSED

If your love doesn't light the lamp
Your love is flawed,
If your mind wanders for materials
Your mind needs to be cured.

WATCH OUT

Those who take life for granted
Life will happen to you,
Sooner or later
Life will show itself to you.

Be still and prepare
Don't slip yourself into illusion,
Cause it's easy loosing
It's painful to regain.

CANNOT QUIT

At times I don't even want to live
For the truth which is not enough,
At times I feel people deserve more
For which I have to pay.

EARTH

For me
He is my backbone
For me
Om is how I breathe.

Let's get out
Let's heal together,
Have faith in your's
Have faith in yourself
Oo men oo women
We can love this world together.

WAKE ME UP

Its been long
Long staying under water,
I know what it felt like to be out
Or maybe I don't remember now.

SENT HERE FOR A REASON

God show me
Am I not merciful
Am I not forgiver,
For what I am being punished
For what I am not being forgiven?

My kindness
Doesn't seem to attract you,
My endless love
Doesn't seem to soften you
But still, I look up for light
Always, I will look up for you.

DESTINY: WHAT WE DO & WHAT WE ARE GIVEN

Maybe the fault is not up there
In the stars,
Perhaps it's in here
In ourselves
That we are destined by the actions
We took
That we become, not by who we are
But what we do.

IF YOU ARE NICE, EVERYTHING WILL BE GOOD

You came in my path
My direction got changed,
You spelled some magic
My heart got replaced.

People change because of you
Some change for you,
I am the one who won't
But I will turn you, for good.

TAKE CONTROL

In life
I use to drive fast
Every time,
It taught me, its calmness
Which will take you far
Not speed.

ALL THE WAY

In my dream, I remember I was walking
Alone through the streets,
Moments were forgotten as I moved further
Pain and joy felt like it never happened,
Walking through the streets.

Struggles were forgotten in time
But scars were not dissolved in air,
When I look back
I don't see anything
But me looking forward.

Because I was moving towards rebirth
I will have new life
Within this life,
As I was walking through the stars.

6

SPIRITUALITY

MOTHER EARTH

By healing others, I forget
I have to heal myself,
By loving others, I remember
Once I loved myself.

I knew it's going to be hard
But what I didn't know
That it's going to be this hard.

This cannot be the end
I am trying to find meaning,
Let me get lost in it
Let me come again.

DO NOT DISTURB/YOUR PEACE

Don't let nobody tell
You are nobody,
Don't let anyone tell
You cannot be somebody.

One day you gotta decide
What your name should provide,
From that day, you are on the tracks
Which leads to the sky.

LIONS ALSO CRY

I broke apart in tears
On the shoulders of my mom,
That was the time
When I needed her the most.

The only time I cried on her
The only time in tears
I don't want to forget
Because that's the comfort I needed,
The hope which I required
The love which she can only provide.

AMRITSAR

Standing there looking at the painting
The old lady beside me, mourning.
With tears for the loved ones
Brutally killed by the British rule,
Innocent people slaughtered
Innocent lives lost,
Just for being innocent
Just for being human.

CHANT LOVE

I close my eyes
I learn,
I open my eyes
I help others with what I learned.
I close my eyes
To learn without bias,
I open my eyes
To help others without being bias.

For me, there are only
Two kinds, Love & Hate
For me I provide
Love, those who love
For me I provide
Love, those who hate.

<u>KETU</u>

I sing her love
For what she has blessed me,
I always lay in her arms
For I know, I will be safe.

ITS COUNTED

What has to happen
Will happen
One way or the other,
Like nature find its way to regenerate
Like nature find its way to destroy.
Every pain needs to be endured
Every pain needs to be cured,
For it is there as a message
Which needs to be matured.

LIFE IS A...

Life is an ocean,
You are on a boat
With devil along you
Ready to eat you
Either you control it
Or get controlled by it.

Life is a canyon
You might get lost
You might get found,
It's a wonder
Not forever
But for a while.

We will get hurt
To realize the value
Of comfort,
There will be failures
To make you strong
But you gotta stay firm as
Life is like a tree.

SELFISH

Selfish is the one
Who kill themselves,
Selfish they are to
Think about themselves
& not for those
Who loves them.

SOMETHING TO TELL YOU

My eyes are all red
Still, I am looking for you
In every corner, every time
Sometimes I stumble upon you
Thinking it's you
But reality saddens me
That it's not you.

I keep searching for
The love I endure
I keep searching that in you
The girl
Where are you?

ONE MORE CUP OF PEACE

What we put
Doesn't come out same,
Life doesn't justify it
But now is not the time
To cry, my girl
Now is not the time
To waste your time my boy.

WE ARE GIFTED

Your heart is the weapon
With bullet of love,
It can hit anyone
It can heal anyone.
For the time is the witness
Its the tool we are given,
Some use it, and some don't
But for you its given
To fulfill the purpose
The purpose of life.

SINGING TO MYSELF

How you feel?
When your world does not match
With the world outside.
How do you feel?
When all you can see is you
All alone in this world.

I AM TIRED

I hope its true what you told me
I hope its true I can overcome anything,
Tell me if I wasn't dedicated enough
Because I am losing hope
Even after giving everything.

GENTLE ANXIETY

I tried too hard
I tried not to cry too hard
But I am a human after all,
How can I change things
Which I don't have power for.

RHYTHM

Life has to be synchronized
Just like love
Real love is being synchronized,
This soul needs to
With the one who created it
& Our only way is faith.

Walk in God's name
He shall perish your pain,
Those who show faith in him
He shows love in them.

PRESS THE SWITCH

Love is infinite
If you love, you will get love back
Not now then in a moment
Love is definite.

You might be on the wrong floor
Or maybe still at ground
But life always goes up
If you do things
Which makes you go up above.

You can run everywhere
But you cannot escape karma,
Its the power which you have
To break you or make you.

STEVE IN SEARCH FOR THE LIGHT

Because of the happenings
I questioned myself
Because of the sufferings
I had to.

Am I not good enough?
Did I do wrongs before I was even born?
I was left alone to find answers
I was searching in the past
Which I don't know
Which was forgotten
When I was born.

I kept looking & searching
I looked up & maybe I found it,
Greatness is coming down
To earth & from it
It's taking away the dark.

Stranger things are bound to happen
Its the way life happens
Either for good or for nothing,
It's up to you.

THE THIRD EYE

You are as wild
As your love,
You honor sex
As you praise honesty.

The creator of everything
Doesn't say sex is sin
Or sex is shameful,
If it was why he blessed us
With this powerful tool.
It is there to proof itself
Sex is the ultimate pleasure
Honor is the key
To unlock the treasure.

WE OWE HIM

I love our God
More than anything,
I try to say
Om & his many names
More than I say, love.

Show me the way
To love you more,
No matter how much I love
I still feel I owe you more.

7

AMBITIONS

FROM WITHIN

I shall defeat them
With kindness
Whoever betrays me,
I shall conquer them
With persistence.
Love me hate me
I shall rise with
Love as my weapon
Pain as my strength,
I shall rise from within.

ANGEL DANCING IN THE RAIN

I guess it all goes down
To the sand
From which we came up,
I guess we are not the only ones
Maybe on earth
Maybe as humans
But we are not the only ones.

IT COMES AND GOES

Everything is corruptible
Everything but light inside you,
Once its enlightened
You will see the light in the world
Which was not there before you.

I was flying in the oceans
Then I was swimming in the skies,
It felt like I was free again
In reality, I wasn't
But still
I felt the power of light...Again.

NEW YORK

New York New York New York
That beautiful girl,
The girl who is hot
Who is wild
That girl that won't let you sleep.
She will keep you in wonder
Day & night
She is the most attractive
Of them all.
NY just don't let me go at all.

I WAS BORN

Where I was born
Where I belong
Not where I come from
But where my soul comes from.

Landed directly onto the feet of God
That day I was born,
Not for comfort
But for lessons.

I am proud of the place I was born
Prouder to go
Where I was born for,
All cause of blessings
Where I was born.

RISE

I

To them, you shall be freak
For you, it should be fine,
To them, the rest will be weak
But it should not define you
It should not stray you.

II

Pain is what defines you
Pain is what made you,
Not alone but only with blessings
Which then turned in favor for you.

III

Blind is he, who cannot see
Lord is what we cannot see,
We all are blind
We all cannot see
Still, those who are willing to look
They see what many can't.

RAHU

Boxing ring of life
Knocked down to the ground,
Where some get up & some don't
Give us strength father.

I seek you in my defeated days
I seek you more in my cherished days,
Father for you I crossed the oceans
It's you who will take me back
Not for rest but for strength.
In the land of the free &
The Home of the brave
I seek your way.

TRAIN

Either
you
jump
in
front
of
the
train
or
jump
on
it.

I

IN HER

I wanna get drown in her eyes
To see what she sees, forever.
I wanna get inside of her
So she can love me now or never.

II

I SEE YOU

You show me the purpose, like
Boundaries make the way
I can see the light
A million miles away.

WAS ALL ALONE, WITH AN ARMY OF FAITH

Too much of anything
Will make you fall,
Like even too much trust
Can make illusions.

Why you are afraid
When God is with you,
Why you will be lonely
When he is there for you

Its been 22 years
You have no idea
What I have been through,
With all those sufferings
One thing was consistent
Me being alone
And still, I made it this far,
As he was with me
As he shall be with me.

PUT YOUR MONEY ON ME

Sometimes I win
Sometimes I learn
But I never lose,

Every little bit
Which hurts,
Every little bit
Which heals,
Makes me win more
Makes me love more
But I never lose.

I WON'T BE AFRAID / 19

I will be
I will be by your side
Like my mother
My mother is always by my side
Like my mother
Who cares for her part,
Part of her body
Part of her soul
No matter what
Even now,
No matter what
I will be by your side.

ABUSE OF POWER

Kings were laying on their comfort
They were asked to serve
But making other's life even worse,

There was a poor man who dared to ask
Why we don't get what we deserve for work??
Why we have to suffer even after work??

Even though the king ignored him
But he cannot ignore his own fate,
For what he has done
Shall come to him in a life or this one,
For what you do
To you, it shall be done.

NEVER ENOUGH

The moment I think I have provided enough
My inner self-whispers Not Yet,
The moment I imagine I can't make it any more
Ocean within me screams NOT YET.

FOR THE BEST

You know the wind blows
But you don't know how it blows
You might not know why it blows.

You just have to flow with it,
Just live through it.

MAKE ME FALL ASLEEP

I use to keep knocking
Knocking the door
The door which is inside of me,
To wake me up
To see the reality
Harsh reality.

Now I don't anymore
Because now I am always awake
To take down the reality
I am born into,
To create the reality
I desire to be.

SONG OF JULY

Every step is noted
No honest work goes to vain
Like no wrong deed goes to hide,

Take his hand
Follow the right path,
No matter what you see
No matter what you face
You should follow the right way,

Then he shall walk with you
Even if you don't need him
He shall be there for you.

I

TO THE WOLVES WHO DREAM

People have to accept it
People will endure it,
First when you learn what's right
For you
They will learn what's wrong
With them.

II

TO THE WOLVES WHO ENDURE

They embrace it
Even when they know what's coming,
There is fear in them
There is the pain in them
Which makes them endure
Which makes them drink
All of it.

III

TO THE WOLVES WHO GO BEYOND

I see the light across the ocean
Shattering over the waves,
Trying to break my point of view
Still, I am standing,
With faith beside me
Faith who took me beyond
Of where I was
Of what I am.

ECHO

The silent heart always speaks louder
Through the oceans, over the mountains
Silent heart echoes in the midst of chaos.

LETTER

To,
Vulnerable (Those Who Love)

Things Don't Go In One Direction
But It Won't Hurt Always
It Doesn't Have To,
That's Against The Universal Creation.
If You Are Broken
Then Its For You To Heal.
You Ended Up Reading This
For Countless Words
You Could Have Read Instead.
So, You Will Be Healed
& You Will Be Saved.

From
Kartikay D Pawar

THE END

THIS BOOK IS DEDICATED TO MY BROTHER

RAHUL THADANI

(MAR 10, 1996 - SEP 21, 2018)

R.I.P
Rahul, my childhood best friend, my brother, my family. I remember our 10 years of friendship which was unbreakable & still is unbreakable. I remember how you helped me grow in life, I remember those days when we tried everything together in life. You always motivated me in my toughest days, you took me out of my dangerous thoughts in 2016, you always believed in me when no one else did. Rahul, you know with you only I use to share what I wanted in my life & you always supported me. I just cannot forget (and I don't want to forget) the last moments I spent with you, I was holding your hand and helped you intake juice with my own hands because I know you were never close to anyone more than me. I was the last one you were able to talk to (even though with full of struggle & short breath) just before you went far away in a place which is way beautiful & painless than this earth.
You will always be there with me in my heart, I am giving you love, blessings & I pray that you are happy up there in the stars.
I love you, always.

P.S
Thanks for being the first person to have this book

(I am glad you approved it)

I AM GRATEFUL TO

MOM and DAD for always encouraging me and loving me when no one else did.

Rahul for always being my brother.

Omkar for always showing me the light and giving positivity like no other.

Rudra for his love.

Mohit for always standing beside me.

Haters for giving me Fierce Motivation.

The ones with whom I shared the love for a short/long duration.

My birth city 'Jodhpur' for embedding the importance of being Grateful.

The USA for teaching me that *Anything is Possible*.

And most importantly all of you, beautiful people who support & share the love for the Life which I am sharing.

ABOUT THE AUTHOR

Kartikay D Pawar a.k.a. 'K.P' is a Writer, Director & Entrepreneur with many International Awards to his name for his Acclaimed Short Films.
He is from India but calls World as his Home.

You can follow his Journey through:
Instagram: @kartikaydpawar
IMDb: Kartikay D Pawar

Share your love with:
#kartikaypoetry #poetrykp #lifeoflotus